Pretty Weddings for
Practically Pennies

Pretty Weddings for Practically Pennies

By Catherine Yarnovich Risling

Sterling Publishing Co., Inc. New York
A Sterling/Chapelle Book

Chapelle, Ltd.:
    Jo Packham, Sara Toliver, Cindy Stoeckl

A Red Lips 4 Courage Book
    Eileen Cannon Paulin, Rebecca Ittner,
    Catherine Yarnovich Risling, Jayne Cosh

Red Lips 4 Courage Communications, Inc.
    8502 E. Chapman Ave., 303
    Orange, CA 92869
    (714) 289-0139
    e-mail: rl4courage@redlips4courage.com
    web site: www.redlips4courage.com

If you have any questions or comments, please contact:
Chapelle, Ltd., Inc., P.O. Box 9252, Ogden, UT 84409
(801) 621-2777 • (801) 621-2788 Fax
e-mail: chapelle@chapelleltd.com
web site: www.chapelleltd.com

Library of Congress Cataloging-in-Publication Data
Risling, Catherine Yarnovich.
Pretty weddings for practically pennies / by Catherine Yarnovich Risling.
    p. cm.
Includes index.
ISBN 1-4027-1348-7
1. Handicraft. 2. Wedding decorations. I. Title.

TT149.R55 2005
745.594'1--dc22

2004018553

10 9 8 7 6 5 4 3 2 1
Published by Sterling Publishing Co., Inc.
387 Park Ave. South, New York, NY 10016
©2005 by Catherine Yarnovich Risling
Distributed in Canada by Sterling Publishing
c/o Canadian Manda Group, 165 Dufferin Street,
Toronto, Ontario, Canada M6K 3H6
Distributed in Great Britain by Chrysalis Books Group PLC,
The Chrysalis Building, Bramley Road, London W10 6SP, England
Distributed in Australia by Capricorn Link (Australia) Pty. Ltd.
P. O. Box 704, Windsor, NSW 2756, Australia
Printed and Bound in China
All Rights Reserved

Sterling ISBN 1-4027-1348-7

Table of Contents

Memories in the Making

A few years ago, I made a commitment to love, honor, and cherish. I also committed myself to saving money in every way possible. As long as I didn't have to sew it or bake it, I wanted to make it.

I was only going to marry once, and I wanted to put great thought into each detail. My soon-to-be husband was patient as I paraded decorative papers, boxes of Jordan almonds, and spools of ribbons in front of him.

My long list of projects began with the save-the-date cards, continued with the party favors and table decorations, and culminated in my much-anticipated days as a bride-to-be with a minute-by-minute wedding day itinerary. The details had to be creative and special, even if that meant photocopying 65 photos of my guests at their own weddings, cropping them to perfect size, and pasting each one onto a piece of pretty paper to be set at each table.

On Friday nights, those weeks and months leading up to our wedding, I could be found diligently gluing layers of handmade paper and ribbon to votive holders and paper tissue holders. My mom and close friends were there to lend support—risking a few hot glue burns in the name of our happiness.

Naturally, I wanted to save money. But I also wanted to be able to look around on my wedding day with pride and smile at the beautiful setting I had created. Others noticed too—graciously pointing out their favorite elements for months afterward.

Our late-afternoon reception was held at a striking Mediterranean-style estate high on a hill with fantastic views. Everything I chose reflected the ambience of the setting—from the warm, subtle colors to the simple elegance in each detail. Our guest list of 130 was not too large, not too small—just right.

For the wedding, I invested money in things that could be reused. For example, a hand-carved 24" by 36" frame became the place card holder with some fabric and ribbon. After the wedding, the glass was inserted back into the frame, which was hung in our living room with a new piece of artwork.

The decorations at the church—paper cones filled with flowers—were transported to the reception to decorate the head table. The topiaries that flanked the church altar took center stage at the reception, where they were wrapped in tulle and placed at the entrance. The 4-foot ivies became thank-you gifts to a sister who lent an immeasurable amount of love and support.

When my mother-in-law revealed one day that she still had her cake topper that was more than three decades old, I was eager to check it out. She unwrapped the gracefully aged topper and I was smitten. I couldn't think of a better way to honor my in-laws, who were celebrating 35 years of marriage the same year we were married.

The year of engagement provided me with ample time to plan and prepare as I scoured books and magazines for cost-saving ideas. Ultimately, the "borrowed" ideas became my own as I tweaked them—some a little, some much more. After the honeymoon had become a distant memory, I realized that those pre-wedding days of watching a vision come true were fond memories in the making.

As you plan your special day, or help someone dear to you get ready for her own, we hope you enjoy the thoughtful ideas provided throughout this book.

Catherine Yarnovich Risling

Dedication

This book is dedicated to my husband, Greg, who makes marriage a blessing every day. And to my family, whose love and honesty led me to marry my best friend.

Introduction

Before You Get Started

The ring is purchased, the date is set, and you've already started shopping for a dress. Now the fun begins!

There are so many wonderful things to plan for a wedding. From picking out favorite flowers to deciding which design will make the cake stand out, your choices can be as subdued—or creatively eclectic—as you wish them to be. There can be vintage barrels outside to hold wedding gifts and lemonade can be served in old-fashioned canning jars for a country-themed reception; or, guest tables with candelabrums entwined with roses will create a more sophisticated affair.

Instead of spending a small fortune on store-bought wedding accessories like the veil, guest book, or party favors, you can be creative and end up with something very special. Simple selections can easily be dressed up with flowers, ribbons, rhinestones, beads, or whatever else strikes your fancy.

This book should inspire you to personalize your wedding in as many ways as you can. But before you hit the aisles of your favorite craft store, some things need to be considered to keep you focused.

(Above) Rather than a large arrangement, a few single stems make a stunning centerpiece. Use a few petals to decorate around the bottom of the vase.

(Opposite page) Make a statement of simple elegance with a bouquet of hand-tied tulips. Long white gloves add a touch of formality.

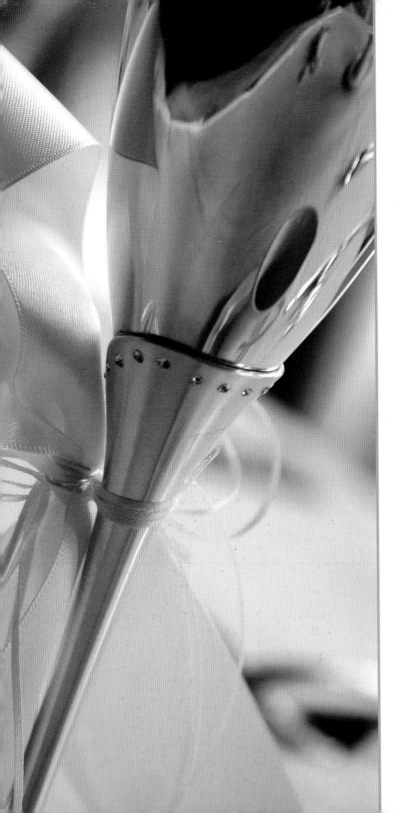

Define Your Style

While there are about as many wedding styles as there are hairstyles, four timeless tastes seem to endure—Romantic, Country, Vintage Chic, and Champagne.

Before choosing the look you want, decide on the location of your wedding festivities. Will they be outside, under a grand old oak amid verdant pastures? Or, have you selected a favorite restaurant with outstanding fare and simple surroundings? The time of year is just as important and can help in deciding on a theme.

A December wedding naturally lends itself to winter whites and twinkling lights. The decorations of the season provide a beautiful backdrop for an elegant evening celebration. The natural tones of autumn are warm and the weather tends to be comfortable, making it a good time for either indoor or outdoor weddings. Summer is a wonderful time to adopt a waterside theme. Tables set with shells and centerpieces with gold-fish are stunning and fun! Don't overlook the season of new beginnings—after all, the most popular time for weddings is spring.

The beauty is in the details, and it doesn't take a cache of cash to achieve the wedding of your dreams.

Define Your Budget

After the location has been chosen, it's time to come up with a budget. Staying on track financially will not only help guide your decisions, it will help alleviate stress during the planning stages. You don't need to skimp on the things that really matter to you. If you pay a little more than you expected for the cake or the entrée, the cost can be offset by spending less on party favors or putting together your own centerpieces.

A memorable wedding doesn't have to come with a steep price tag. Discard "the sky's the limit" attitude. What makes a wedding truly special are the details and the way you've drawn your guests into the event. Remember, they are your guests, there to toast you and your spouse.

(Above) Little details are often noticed at a wedding. If you take the time to decorate the cake knife and server you will be happy you did when the wedding photos arrive.

(Opposite page) Beautiful toasting goblets can be a decorative element on the cake table, and will become an heirloom long after the wedding.

Bride Ideas
Eye on Expenses

When setting a budget, begin with what matters most and work backwards. If flowers are most important or your dress must be designer-made and off-the-rack has been banished from your vocabulary, allow the appropriate amount in your budget for these things. Just remember, you'll have to save in other places. Other expenses to consider:

- Bride and bridal party: Dress, shoes, accessories, flowers, gifts, ring

- Decorations: Party favors, centerpieces, chair embellishments

- Entertainment: DJ or band

- Food and beverages: Sit down or buffet, alcohol-free or soft drinks only, cake

- Groom and groomsmen: Boutonnieres, tuxedos, gifts, ring

- Photographer and videographer: Before and during wedding and reception

- Setting: Day or evening wedding, inside or out, length of festivities

- Stationery: Save-the-date cards, invitations, menus, place cards, thank-you cards

Define Your Time

It would be wonderful if you could build your own white gazebo and take your vows beneath it. But realistically, who has the ability or the time?

From the day after the engagement until the day before the nuptials, engaged couples are living with deadlines. There are so many decisions to be made, and if you hope to save money, there also will be many things to make. If you plan wisely, and accept offers of help from your family and friends, things will go much smoother.

It's never too early to start preparations. The earlier you begin, the more time you have to wait for items to go on sale and to comparison shop. After all, the name of the game is to save money—and to have the wedding of your dreams.

(Right) Once thrown at the bride and groom in a tradition of good luck, rice serves to hold candles in a glass vase. Having each guest hold a lit candle during the send-off is a romantic touch.

(Opposite page) A simple white-frosted cake can be dressed up with fresh flowers and berries. No one says it has to be white-on-white. If you are passionate about pink flowers, enjoy them on your wedding cake.

Bride Ideas
Easy Cost Cuts

If you decide to spend a large portion of your budget on a band at the reception, or serving a six-course meal, you'll definitely be looking for ways to cut costs. Some options to consider:

- Use the offset printing process instead of costly thermograph engraving for your invitations.

- Silk or dried flowers may be used sparingly to accent bridal or bridesmaid bouquets—no one will ever know the difference.

- Decorate your reception tables with loose flowers rather than elaborate centerpieces.

- Store-bought cakes can be just as elegant as costly custom-made ones when adorned with edible flowers or ribbon.

- Rather than calligraphy, print your own menu cards, table numbers, and place cards from your home computer. Be sure to use a quality laser printer.

(Top) Simple touches such as the decoration of the flower girl's basket lend a festive mood to an already beautiful day.

(Above) The flowers on the guest book table can do double duty if you ask an attendant to whisk them from the wedding ceremony to the receiving table at the reception.

(Opposite page) A fondant wedding cake is a beautiful statement by itself. A simple scattering of flower petals around the base is just enough to decorate the table.

Chapter One

Modern Romance

Today's romantic wedding styles are blooming with color, style, and a hint of the extraordinary.

Remember the days of old, when wedding dresses and bridal bouquets seemed to blend together into one pleasant, but bland, memory? Boutonnieres were almost always white roses and party favors were inevitably pillow dinner mints or matchbooks inscribed with the bride and groom's names and wedding date. The cake was simple, white, and there was usually a traditional champagne fountain nearby.

Today, weddings are all about romance and showing your favorite colors. Just about anything goes when it comes to the details, and the more sweet and unique, the better.

(Left) A candelabrum abloom with fresh flowers and topped with handmade paper shades makes a sentimental and eclectic centerpiece.

(Opposite page) Keeping your guest list small may enable you to spend more on the quality and details of the event. Intimate tables of four are festive when layered with colorful table linens and an abundance of spring flowers.

Save the Date

A prelude to the wedding invitation is the save-the-date announcement that includes details of the upcoming nuptials. This is less formal than the wedding invitation and can be fun to design and send out.

With so many beautiful decorative papers–both handmade and scrapbook style–there's no limit to what you can come up with. Your words can be formal or light-hearted, and remember that a simple card can be embellished with beads, ribbon, or just about anything else you prefer.

If you choose a one-sided announcement, consider layering papers for a rich effect, and top them off with a ribbon tied through punched holes. It's a simple yet attractive look that requires cutting paper, printing the announcement and tying a pretty bow.

(Right top) There are so many ways to ask your guests to save the date–and so many fonts from which to choose. A red border adds color to the card, while a delightful photograph of the engaged couple doesn't leave anyone guessing who's getting married.

(Right bottom) By printing the details on the back of the card, you'll save money and time.

Please Save the Date

July 17th

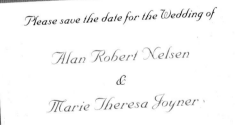

Please save the date for the Wedding of

Alan Robert Nelsen

&

Marie Theresa Joyner

Country Inn and Suites
(800) 456-4000
ask for Nelsen/Joyner party for
discounted rates

Invitations to Follow

www.alanandmarie.com

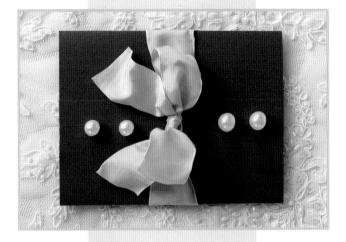

Wedding Invitations

When Jeanne and Cory Baumann were engaged, they knew they wanted to set their own tone. That meant no wedding bells, hearts, or other cutesy signature accents found on store-bought wedding invitations.

A friend designed a sophisticated invitation embellished with their first-name initials at the top and a wonderful inviting message. The invitation is accented with pearls on the front and tied with a bow, a dynamic presentation that beautifully leads the guest to what's inside.

(Left top and bottom) The investment of time assembling invitations can result in a designer look at a fraction of the cost. A non-traditional twist to a wedding invitation marries the formality of a tuxedo with the sophistication of pearls, all tied up with a bow and waiting to reveal the details of the celebration.

Using In-Season Flowers

Flying in roses from Ecuador or tulips from Holland is very expensive, so be sure to choose flowers that are local and in season. Here is a look at flowers typically available by season:

Spring

Tulip, iris, daffodil, ranunculus, delphinium, freesia, larkspur, peony, viburnum, heather, genista, waxflower, and Queen Anne's lace.

Summer

Rose, lily, gerbera, snapdragon, sweet pea, hydrangea, stephanotis, bouvardia, and astilbe.

Late Summer, Early Fall

Chrysanthemum, aster, dahlia, sunflower, yarrow, bird of paradise, amaranthus, celosia, and gloriosa.

Winter

Cymbidium, dendrorobium, amaryllis, oriental lily, agapanthus, euphorbia, and berries including hypericum, pepperberry, and holly.

Bridal Bouquets

A timeless bouquet is all white, but that doesn't mean your bouquet has to be traditional. Just about any flowers these days can be clustered together to form a bouquet. With some full green leaves as background accents, or maybe a few stems of stephanotis, the bouquet can bring lots of color or subtle interest.

When choosing a bouquet, consider flowers that don't bruise easily and will withstand a day with little water. Roses make gorgeous arrangements, but alternatives such as tulips are just as dashing. Consider a simple hand-tied arrangement of stems, or a bouquet filled with just a few hand-picked roses and lots of filler flowers.

(Above) When it comes to bridal bouquets, often less is more. A tight grouping of flowers is elegant and easy to handle throughout the day. Try to choose hearty flowers such as roses or tulips.

(Opposite page) Wrapping the stems of the flowers with a simple white ribbon keeps hands clean and gives the bouquet a finished look. Consider leaving a bit of the stems open so that the bouquet can rest in a small amount of water until right before the ceremony begins.

Easy-to-Make Boutonnieres

Boutonniere flowers are typically chosen from the flowers in the bride's bouquet.

Materials:

- Accent flowers (optional)
- Corsage pin
- Green floral tape
- One or two flowers of choice
- Ribbon
- Thin floral wire

To make:

1. Cut stems 3"-4" long.

2. Arrange flowers, adding accent flowers if desired.

3. Secure stems together with thin floral wire.

4. Place green tape at bottom of stems, underneath flowers, and roll while stretching tape around stems.

5. Wrap ribbon around floral tape to cover, or tie in a bow.

Boutonnieres

A boutonniere takes endless well-intentioned abuse on a wedding day. While delicate stephanotis and a miniature cream rose ensemble looks spectacular at first, it quickly wilts after countless hugs from well-wishers. Sometimes it's inevitable, but choosing a hardy flower will help stave off "the droops."

Another way to preserve the groom's boutonniere is to opt for silk or dried flowers such as lavender in spring, or berries if it's a winter wedding. Rather than wrap the flower in floral tape, consider a French ribbon or elegant piece of fabric. With so many dry and silk choices available, you can pin just about any lasting bloom on a lapel.

(Opposite page, clockwise from top left) A single lavender tulip tied with a bit of raffia makes a simple statement. Combine small faux flowers with ribbon to make a boutonniere that looks like a miniature bouquet. Three delicate hyacinths and a small piece of sea grass are a sweet statement on a lapel. Vintage ribbon used to accent small ceramic flowers makes a boutonniere guaranteed to last throughout the day.

Bride Ideas
Making a Flower Girl Halo

Materials:

- Flowers
- Pipe cleaners
- Ribbons
- White floral tape

To make:

1. Cover 2 pipe cleaners with floral tape. Starting at top of first pipe cleaner, hold with one hand and twist tape around it.

2. When you get to bottom of first pipe cleaner, twist the next one to it and continue taping.

3. Twist remaining two pipe cleaner ends together to form the halo base.

4. Starting in one place, take 1" cluster of flowers and hold it against wreath base. Cover stems with floral tape. As you progress, cover previous stems with next bunch of flowers.

5. Continue all around halo base. Cover end of stem pieces with ribbon.

6. Tie bow and allow streamers to hang down back of halo.

Flower Girl Accents

Little girls love to dress up, and a wedding is the perfect day to do just that. They are a sweet part of the ceremony, lending a beacon of good luck and cheer. It's fun to add some special touches for girls to wear and carry.

A halo of flowers is a fresh alternative to headbands and barrettes, and it is easy to make. The flowers can mirror those in the bridal bouquet, and the entire piece can be wrapped and tied with ribbon.

(Above) A delicate flower halo is a sweet crown for the flower girl princess-for-a-day.

(Opposite page) Rather than spending money on expensive flowers for petals, recruit friends and family members to gather garden roses and break the blooms apart to fill the flower girl's delicate basket.

Bride Ideas
Making a Headband Veil

Materials:

- Accents such as silk flowers, pearls, beads, etc.
- Glue gun and glue sticks
- Pre-made veil (available at many craft stores)
- White glue
- White headband

To make:

1. Attach the veil to the headband according to instructions on veil package.

2. Hot glue flowers to the center of the band, starting with bigger flowers.

3. Fill in all holes around and in between flowers with smaller flowers and/or accents with white glue. If desired, mix in rhinestones and pearls.

(Top right and opposite page) Since the soft netting of a bridal veil is a statement in itself, consider a very simple headpiece such as an embellished headband.

Bridal Veils

Traditionally it was believed that brides were vulnerable to evil spirits. The veil originates with ancient Roman brides, who wore the headpiece to disguise and outwit the demons. According to Jewish custom, the veil is lowered after the groom looks at the bride to confirm her identity.

While veils are steeped in tradition, their meaning is less ominous these days. A veil makes a bride feel like royalty on her wedding day, and the best part is it can be worn with many different hairstyles. A veil can be attached to a headband, hair clips, or combs. It's best to closely match the hue of the netting to the bridal gown, whether it is white, ivory, or cream. A simple headband can be embellished with silk flowers and the veil itself accented with pearls or beading.

Receiving Table

First impressions are priceless. Typically, the first thing guests see when they arrive at the reception is the receiving table. It is a great place to set out your guest book, an engagement photo, and seating assignments. Add a plate of sweets or a dish of mints for your guests' refreshment. If gifts are going to be placed on this table, be sure there is plenty of space.

Set with a white tablecloth, shimmering organza, layers of tulle or simply bare, the table can be round, square rectangular—whatever you prefer. The receiving table doesn't have to be elaborate to be a warm greeting as guests enter the reception.

(Top left, left, and opposite page) A receiving table is a quiet greeting to guests entering a wedding reception. Put some special thought into this first impression by providing a sweet treat for refreshment, a greeting, and plenty of room to hold gifts.

33

Place Card Holders

Beautifully inscribed place cards are a wonderful way to show guests to their seats and can become a keepsake of the special day. After all the effort to create them, they deserve a lovely display. While place cards can be lined up on a table, there are other choices that strike a more creative chord.

Consider using a three-tier dessert tray for displaying place cards. Embellishments such as trim and flowers can turn it into a spectacular display, adding color and interest to an otherwise plain space.

If you arrange the place cards several rows deep, be sure there is enough space for guests to easily read and remove their card. If more room is needed, arrange the spillover on a nearby table.

(Right and opposite page) A three-tier cake stand can be embellished with beaded trim and small faux flowers attached with a glue gun. The three levels are a wonderful way to array place cards. Each card can be adorned with dried or silk flowers.

Pretty Place Cards

When it comes to paper, the prettier the better. Who can settle for plain cards when there are so many ways to dress them up? Card stock is available for traditional place cards, or innovative ones can be fashioned from textured, handmade, or other decorative papers.

While calligraphy is a traditional choice for place cards, it is also the more costly one. You can create the look of calligraphy by choosing the right font on a computer. By printing, cutting, and folding the cards you'll save the cost of a custom job. Names can be printed on clear matte labels and affixed to the place cards as another option.

(Left) Rather than using mundane numbers, name tables for places that are special to you and have the place card direct guests to the right location.

(Opposite page, from top left) Decorative scrapbooking scissors and paper embellishments can be used to create delicate place cards. Punching a hole and threading a ribbon through the top gives a custom look and adds dimension. Large novelty paper punches are available in a variety of cutouts including an engagement ring. Gluing on a few rhinestones adds a little glitz. Combining rubber stamps and ribbon is another way to add personalization to place cards.

Bride Ideas
Ribbon Roses

Materials:

- 22" length of wired ribbon (the wider the ribbon, the bigger the rose)

To make:

1. Remove wire from one side of ribbon.

2. Make knot at one end of ribbon. At opposite end, poke out wire from one side.

3. Loosely gather ribbon along this wire down to the knot. Don't pull too hard—it could snap.

4. Continue gathering until entire side is ruffled and curling naturally. Leave wire end free; do not cut.

5. Form rose by holding knotted end in one hand and begin to spiral gathered ribbon around knot loosely with other hand.

6. Wrap tightly at first to form a "bud," then continue wrapping lightly so that it flares out and acquires an open rose effect.

7. At end, fold raw edge down to meet gathered edge. Secure by wrapping wire length around knot tightly and catching in free end; cut wire end off.

8. Adjust "petals" to create desired effect.

Centerpiece Ideas

While flowers are one of the more costly items in a wedding budget, there are many ways to cut cost without sacrificing impact. Smaller containers hold fewer flowers and leaves and other greenery can be used as filler. Store-bought vases also can be a big expense. Shop a local dollar store for bargain vases that can be transformed.

A plain vase can become dazzling by wrapping it with fabric and accenting it with strips of ribbon and hand-made ribbon roses. You can carry the theme by using the same décor on votive holders to complement the vases. Loose flowers are easily arranged and don't require a florist's expertise. It's all in the presentation…and the details.

(Above) Make coordinating votive candle holders using the same fabric as the vases. Trim the holders with ribbon flowers you make yourself.

(Opposite page) When grouping the flower-filled vase with votive holders, work in groups of three—odd numbers are more pleasing to the eye.

Bride Ideas
Craft a Wedding Wreath

Materials:

- 12" floral foam base (craft stores sell them in many shapes and sizes)
- Bunches of flowers
- Floral tape
- Foliage
- Ribbon
- Wire or fishing line

To make:

1. Immerse floral foam base in water until it is wet, but not fully saturated.

2. Insert foliage first. Keep stems short and cover base with foliage.

3. Insert flowers, spacing them evenly around base.

4. Affix ribbon to back of frame for hanging.

(Above right) A wreath made from colorful spring flowers announces the importance of the big day when hung in greeting on a garden gate.

(Opposite page) While the beauty of a garden itself is a perfect setting for a wedding, small touches like a heart-shaped wreath stand out and will be appreciated by guests.

Reception Décor

It is an old Greek tradition to hang a wreath of fresh flowers on a door to celebrate an occasion. Whether a wedding celebration is near a wooded stream, or in a backyard, wreaths are a wonderful way to dress up a reception.

Flower wreaths make beautiful arrangements that can be hung anywhere, including fences and trees in addition to a front door or gate. They can be suspended by ribbon, attached with strong wire, or hung from a hook. You can either work with a pre-shaped floral base, or easily shape heavy wire into a heart, square, or circle.

Rather than live flowers, consider artificial flowers or interspersing live and silk blooms in the wreath. Before you call a florist, think about what you can make and the savings will follow.

Party Favors

Sometimes the more simple a favor is, the more elegant it becomes. Filling clear cases with all-white almonds and tying them together with a ribbon in the wedding colors is easy to do. When grouped together in a decorative bowl, the impact of the treats together becomes a decoration in itself.

Almonds and other hard shell candies are available in colors other than white, and when displayed in clear jars, they become an edible décor statement. If you intend for guests to help themselves, provide a small scoop or spoon.

Gathering family and bridesmaids together to help assemble favors is a wonderful way to spend time visiting and reviewing the ceremony and reception details.

(Right) Simple heart-shaped favor boxes filled with Jordan almonds are pretty when displayed in a decorative bowl. Guests can help themselves as they leave.

(Opposite page) While white almonds are traditional, there is no rule that says a little color isn't welcome. Order custom colors online, and serve them from large apothecary jars with a spoon.

Bride Ideas
Choosing Candles

Before you settle on inexpensive candles, remember the old adage: you get what you pay for.

Some things to keep in mind:

- Natural waxes burn longer than paraffin wax.

- In general, fragrant candles come with a higher price tag.

- Tapers typically burn faster and often leave a pile of wax at their base.

- Tea lights generally stay lit 4-5 hours. Be sure to choose the ones set in a metal container to easily remove from votive holder.

- Votive candles can last up to 15 hours, while thick pillar candles will last two or three weddings.

- Cold candles burn slower.

Votive Holders

Votive candles provide a soft touch of light and make a lovely favor. They can be lit during the party for ambience and taken home as a remembrance of a special day. While you may be tempted to cut costs on the type of candles you use, be sure to test the burning time before the wedding. Inexpensive candles tend to melt very quickly and won't last long enough to have an impact. Be sure that they are of good enough quality to make it through the reception.

Whether you choose to decoupage paper or lace to a glass holder or wrap a printed piece of vellum around it, there is a craft technique to suit your style and budget.

(Opposite page, from top left) Dried flowers and handmade papers can be adhered to glass with a decoupage medium; for a vintage feel, use a decoupage medium that is intentionally yellowed. Etching cream is available at any craft store and can easily transform a glass holder. Rub-on transfers are a quick way to add a floral motif to glass; trim the top of the holder with beaded ribbon. Layering ribbon and artificial flowers makes a pretty impact.

Wedding Cakes

The early wedding cake was typically a simple, single-tier plum cake. Tastes have come a long way! Today, for anyone with a sweet tooth, the cutting of the cake is an anticipated tradition.

Most modern-day cakes are large and as the guest list grows, so does the number of tiers. Cakes can be works of art themselves. Many brides are introducing color to layers of cake that have traditionally been white. Gorgeous fresh flowers can encircle the tiers or can be tucked in between layers where ample space is provided, thanks to heightened support columns. If you long for sugar flowers, make your way to the cake and candy making aisle at the craft store, where you will find many types of preformed flowers and molds.

With a little imagination and attention to detail, your cake can be as sweet on the outside as it is on the inside.

(Right) Fresh flowers are more practical than those made from frosting because they can be added to a cake after it has been transported, reducing the risk of damaging frosted buds.

(Opposite page) While detailed frosting embellishments are sometimes best left to the pros, the tips needed for decorating a wedding cake are readily available. If you have a friend who decorates cakes, consider asking her to create your cake as a wedding gift.

Chapter Two

Country Charm

Nature lends a stunning backdrop—and some natural ingredients—for a special wedding day.

There's something wonderful about the outdoors—the feel of a soft breeze and the scent and beauty of natural surroundings. In the right season and climate, an outdoor wedding is delightful.

By choosing an outdoor location, the sky is your canopy, and there are many decorating possibilities that lend themselves to a country feel—and what's great is that you don't even need to be in the country.

Elements are typically more natural—wicker baskets, large barrels, just-picked flowers, and inspiration from Mother Nature dress the scene. You can let go of formality and embrace everything that speaks comfort and ease.

Handmade touches—from traditional country to French country—are all at home at an outdoor wedding.

(Left) Hanging tulle from tree trunks is an inexpensive and whimsical way to dress a path or driveway.

(Opposite page) A garden gazebo speaks country charm. Vinyl gazebos can be rented and assembled on site. Consider wrapping the posts with artificial green garland and tucking fresh flowers in small water tubes every few inches.

Save the Date

Many brides are ascribing to the "simpler is better" approach, and save-the-date announcements are a great place to start.

Begin by printing the information you want to share on a sheet of white cardstock, cut to size to fit inside a folded square enclosure that is secured with a glue stick. Seal the envelope with a small dried daisy to hint at the country theme of the wedding. By creating a one-sided document, you are not only saving money, you are saving time.

We're getting married!

Save the date

Caroline and Joseph

June 18, 2005

(Above and right) If you design your save-the-date card to fit inside a folded standard 12" x 12" piece of scrapbook paper, you will be able to choose from a wide variety of papers to use as an envelope.

Wedding Invitations

Once the pre-wedding announcements are sent out, you can then focus on the actual wedding invitation.

We borrowed elements from the save-the-date card when creating this very sweet invitation, including the paper material and the dried daisies. A piece of raffia ties up the entire piece and provides the ideal finishing touch.

Since this invitation is anything but traditional, be as creative and casual with the wording as you'd like.

Caroline Suzanne Marshall
and
Joseph Paul Taylor
Wish for the presence
of your friendship and love
as they exchange vows
Saturday, June 18, 2005
Ceremony begins at 3 pm
Garden Reception to follow

96 Clapboard Way
ton, Massachusetts

(Above and right) The invitation for a country wedding can be as casual as the day it is announcing. Handmade papers and dried flowers along with a raffia bow all add to the ambience of the day.

Bridal Bouquets

Many florists are foregoing the flower market and heading to open fields, woods, and meadows for inspiration. Leaves, berries, twigs, and flowers, gathered loosely together, create a warm, summery feel.

The fresh colors and wonderful fragrance of wildflowers are ideal for bridal bouquets as they lend a relaxed, just-gathered look. Tuck in herbs such as rosemary, which means remembrance, and enjoy the aroma all day.

When it comes to the great outdoors, more is better. Feel free to work with lots of color, and negate the theory that everything should match.

(Top right) A single gathering of calla lilies is an intriguing choice.

(Right) Using the same flowers in a tight arrangement is a graceful statement. If a rose bouquet is made two days before the wedding and stored properly, roses will open for a more country feel.

(Opposite page) Delicate peonies are a classic choice of blooms, especially when clustered together to form a bridal bouquet.

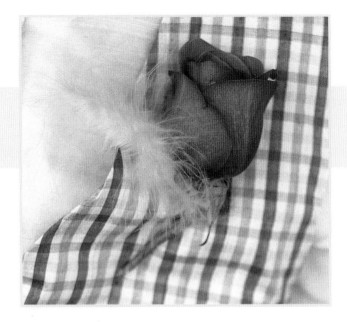

Bride Ideas
Boutonniere Basics

Flower boutonnieres are typically worn by the men in the wedding party, including groomsmen and the fathers of the bride and groom. Some other things to know:

- Boutonnieres are worn over the heart on the left lapel and never with a hankie.

- Traditionally, the groom's boutonniere is different from those worn by the rest of the wedding party and should complement the bridal bouquet.

- A single flower is basic, but double flowers can be used for more formal weddings.

- Keep it simple; elaborate boutonnieres with multiple buds or big flowers tend to look feminine.

(Opposite page, from top left) Small paper flowers trimmed with ribbon and a beaded accent are sure to withstand many hugs and embraces throughout the wedding day. Fresh hydrangea is a classic country flower that mixes well with other flowers. White ribbon flowers make a classic boutonniere. If the bride selects calla lilies for her bouquet, consider using the same flowers for the boutonniere.

Boutonnieres

For an interesting boutonniere, think texture. And for a durable boutonniere, think artificial.

Just as the styles of bridal bouquets change with the times, so do boutonnieres. In fact, flower choices often change with the seasons. With nature's abundance as a limitless resource, all sorts of flowers, herbs, berries, and leaves can be arranged for a one-of-a-kind boutonniere.

Artificial or dried choices can be combined with live elements, and will offer more resilience, which is especially important if the festivities are outdoors and the sun is beaming. With artificial or dried flowers, the boutonnieres can be made ahead of time.

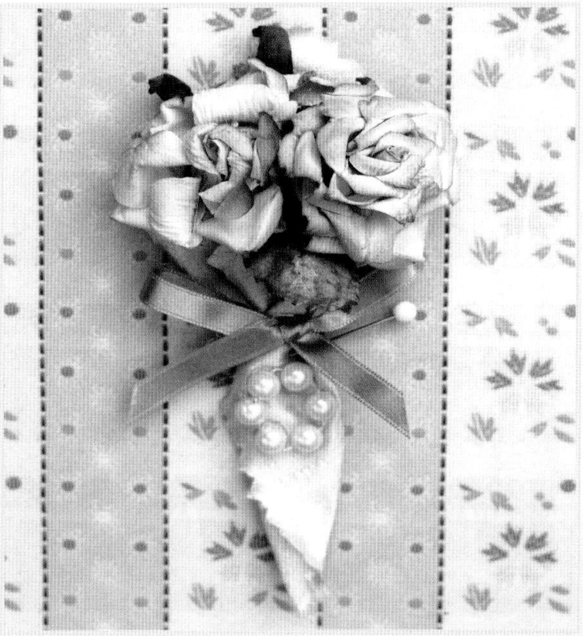
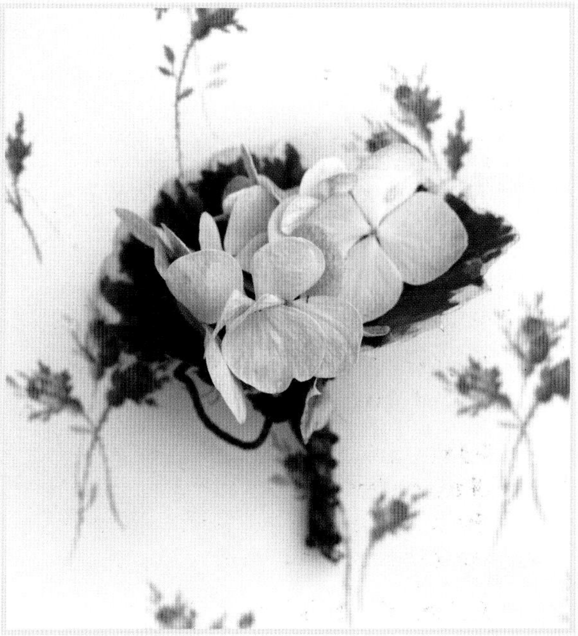
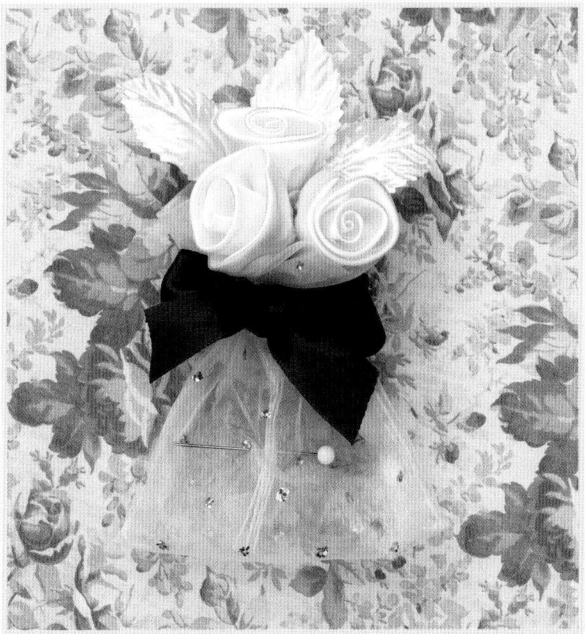
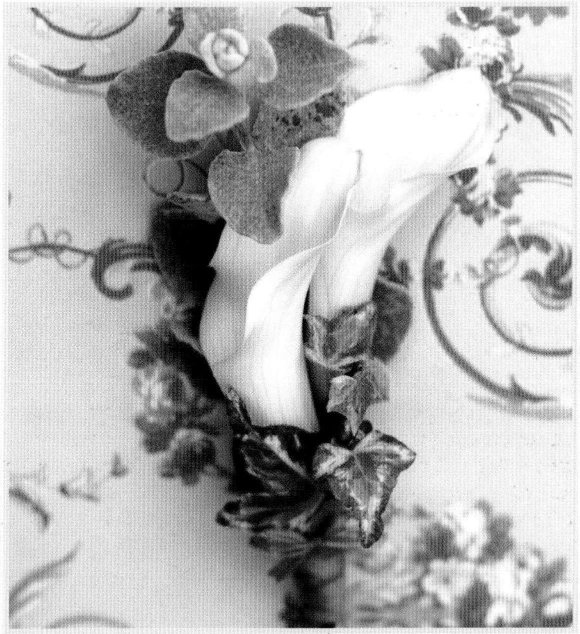

Flower Girl Accents

Since the flower girl will undoubtedly be carrying fresh flowers or petals, she will need an attractive way to hold them. In this case, just about any small basket will do. Pretty lace fabric may be used to cover the basket, or a spray of white paint can soften its look. It also is fun to incorporate some of your young miss' favorite things be they butterflies, big flowers, or feather trim.

Ring Bearer Pillow

Who doesn't love a little boy dressed up, ready to make his way down the aisle? For his big responsibility, a pillow adorned with special embellishments can coordinate with what the flower girl is wearing, or holding.

Simple, white pillows are available in numerous styles and are just waiting for a little creative attention. The pillow will make a lovely keepsake on your bed later.

(Top right) Wispy marabou feathers glued around the rim of the flower girl's basket are a whimsical touch. Look for feather boas in many colors at the craft store.

(Right) Tie or glue a few flowers to the streamers on the flower halo to be worn by the flower girl so she is as cute going as she is coming.

(Opposite page) Embellish the ring pillow to coordinate with the flower girl's accessories by adding flower petals and ribbon streamers.

Bridal Veils

Dressing up a veil can be as simple—or as detailed—as you make it. Choose a headband or wreath on which to attach the veil, or nothing at all, opting for hairpins or combs.

For a veil that is sure to last the whole day—and into the night—attach tulle to a wreath of artificial flowers. At the back, incorporate some flowers in blush hues for subtle color, keeping the primary color of the veil white. If your dress is cream or ivory, a veil in that same color is recommended.

Go a step further by sprinkling the length of the veil with the same blush flowers, leaving a trail of blooms. Just be sure the embellishments do not compete with the gown.

(Right and opposite page) Veils are available in the wedding section of craft stores and can be embellished with silk petals, pearls, and rhinestones.

Chair Décor

A sight to behold, outdoor ceremonies lean on nature to do most of the decorating. Tree-lined pathways and green, rolling hills provide a stunning backdrop. Once chairs are arranged, there are a few more things you can do to create a sense of intimacy.

Tulle is an inexpensive choice of fabric that adds instant beauty when wrapped around trees or tied to the backs of chairs in a swag fashion. Instead of a chair cover, take a 6' length of tulle and tie it around the chair back, finishing it off with a big bow.

At the end of each row, or on the individual seats themselves, a paper cone embellished with ribbon makes a welcoming pocket for fresh flowers, especially ones cut from the garden of a generous guest.

(Right) Paper cones make a lovely decoration especially when combined with tulle on the back of a chair or at the end of a row.

(Opposite page) Before placing flowers in a paper cone, be sure to fill a small plastic bag with water and wrap it closed with a rubber band. This preserves the flowers and keeps the cone from becoming wet.

Fresh is Best

When working with fresh flowers, be sure to select blooms that are full of life, free of insects, and boasting healthy leaves. Some other things to consider:

- Prolong the life of flowers by keeping them in containers that have been cleaned with a mild bleach solution then rinsed well with water before use.

- Be sure flowers have plenty of fresh air. Store in a well-ventilated area free of smoke and car fumes.

- Warm water opens buds and closes flowers, while cool temperatures slow down development, adding longevity to the arrangement. Excessive temperatures damage flowers.

- Floral preservatives, available at florist shops and craft stores, keep a flower's energy level high and inhibit the growth of bacteria, which can reduce the flower's water intake.

Centerpiece Ideas

Whether flowers are fresh from a florist, or gathered from a garden or field, think natural and country-fresh when creating a centerpiece.

While a multi-layered arrangement is stunning, a handful of fresh flowers randomly placed in a glass vase can be just as pretty, especially if the reception is in a vineyard or other informal outdoor setting.

A country arrangement of assorted blooms can incorporate additional elements of nature such as grapevine and wicker. The textures are interesting and the color instantly brightens the table.

Still, a loose arrangement showcases color as well. A clear vase borrows from the floral hues when small decorative elements are painted onto the vase—making the centerpiece a thoughtful take-home gift for special helpers.

(Opposite page) A variety of color including lavender, purple, and yellow are right at home in a country wedding centerpiece. Use curly willow branches for texture and height.

Bridal Showers

You won't be giving your own bridal shower, but friends and family may ask you for a few ideas of what you would like.

Since there are fewer guests at a bridal shower than the actual wedding, there may be more time to spend on the details of the invitations.

If you love French Country, draw on elements that connect with the Old World—old herb crocks, lavender, and home cooking.

A taste of Provencal inspires an invitation tucked inside a small crock adorned with French writing—on its lid is a charming label. The invitation is written on one long piece of artist's paper that measures 1" x 15." This is just enough space to include the pertinent details including time, date, place, and response information.

Once the invite is tucked inside, the jar is filled with dried lavender for a presentation that's both original and aromatic. The jar can be reused to spread fragrance throughout the receiver's home.

(Left) A beautifully lettered scroll is a welcome invitation to any party. There are numerous computer fonts that mimic the art of calligraphy.

(Opposite page) A small French clay herb pot holds the invitation to a bridal shower. The pots are available in gourmet cooking stores.

Kitchen Party

If a bridal shower has a kitchen gift-giving theme, send a culinary-inspired invitation.

A lovely miniature book embellished with water-color illustrations, measuring about 1½" x 2", announces the shower and all the details. A small hole has been punched at the corner, making it easy to thread through a piece of raffia and attach the book invite to a bottle of balsamic vinegar.

An invitation this creative will undoubtedly inspire guests to search out their own cookbooks and whip up a delicious meal at home. The thoughtful invitation sends the party favor before the party, and makes a memorable request that's hard to pass up.

(Left) A small booklet tells guests all they need to know about an upcoming kitchen-themed shower.

(Opposite page) While this invitation may need to be hand delivered, the balsamic vinegar inside the bottle is well worth the effort and makes a lovely gift for guests.

Recipe Party

Lavender is an all-time favorite, for good reason. The dried flowers from this European plant are used in cooking, lotions, aromatherapy, and throughout the home to add fragrance.

An aromatic invite is hand written in calligraphy on a velum envelope filled with dried lavender. The envelopes are then attached to a piece of floral stationery reminiscent of Provencal fabric.

Any bride will welcome a call for recipe cards. She may not know how to cook, but she'll be appreciative when guests share family recipes. The recipe cards echo the French theme, featuring the word recipe in French and a watercolor of lavender on the stationery. Add instructions in the invitation so everyone is sure to fill out the recipe cards properly and bring them to the party.

Recette (RECIPE)

Contribute to a Recipe Book with a recipe for food OR how to live "joie de vivre". 2 pages provided for you here. You may add more paper ~ please write on only one side. Return to Joanna by January

bon appétit ~

(Right) If you provide guests with attractive recipe cards and ask them to bring favorite recipes to a kitchen shower, the bride will receive a thoughtful and priceless gift.

(Opposite page) Consider enclosing sprigs of dried lavender to create the feel and aroma of a country wedding when sending party invitations.

Please give us the pleasure

for to come to

Meredith & Colby

at a

Bridal Luncheon in Provence

Saturday, Janvier 26, 2002

12 noon

27 Moccasin Lane

Rolling Hills Estates, California

Gifts Table Top

Répondez s'il vous plaît stops

by June 10 • Ellen 000 555 0000

Mrs. Torree S
Skylark
de Caza, C

9   2

Party Favors

Craft stores have many wonderful boxes, baskets, and other small containers for party favors. While they may seem a bit plain and unimpressive at first, you can find everything you need to dress up these small trinket holders just an aisle or two over.

Handmade paper gift boxes can be covered with fabric or simply painted, and adorned with ribbon and small artificial flowers. Be as elaborate as you like, and fill the box with just about anything—from candy to fresh flower petals.

A shiny round box can be spray painted and adorned with tiny embellishments. Miniature silver baskets and heart-shaped boxes can be trimmed with ribbons, with pearl trim and flowers attached with a glue gun.

If it's a tasty treat you envision, consider a day or two in the kitchen making cookies for your guests. Tucked in a cellophane bag and tied with a pretty bow, these treats will leave a lasting impression—and a few crumbs for certain—at the end of wedding festivities.

(Left) A sweet cookie surprise is a welcome party favor. Check the cooking aisle of a craft store for easy ideas for decorating and frosting cookies and other treats.

(Opposite page, from top left) Shiny silver favor boxes can be painted flat white and embellished with paper flowers for a classic country look. Small boxes can be dressed up with ribbon roses and trims that match the wedding colors. White heart-shaped favor boxes have endless decorative possibilities, including ribbon, trims, beads, and flowers. Miniature baskets are ready for the occasion with flowers and ribbon.

Wedding Cakes

A simple wedding cake—whether one tier or three, homemade or fresh from a bakery—can take on the flavor of its surroundings with a few select, well-placed blooms. When celebrating in the country style, a simple cake is in order. Consider decorating the cake with the same type of flowers you chose for the bouquet.

Flowers can encircle the cake at its base, decorate each layer, or, when bundled closely together, can serve as the cake topper. Flowers that are not edible should be removed prior to serving.

If you find that some of the flowers have broken or become separated, scatter the loose petals around the base of the cake for scent and sentiment.

(Right) Nothing says country more than daisies and this cake is sure to celebrate that "He Loves Me..." Adorn the cake table with fresh flowers to complement those on the cake.

(Opposite page) Fresh flowers in a variety of colors are a beautiful way to decorate a cake. Because adding flowers cuts down on the amount of labor necessary to decorate the cake, it is a good way to stretch your budget.

Chapter Three

Vintage Traditions

The familiar words of "Something old, something new" set the tone for a wedding with heirloom touches.

You may not wear a Victorian gown or carry a nosegay, and your reception may not be held at an old manor, but that doesn't mean you can't slip in a few vintage touches to convey very special meanings.

There are many traditional elements that can add a hint of old-fashioned charm to a wedding day. They can be as subtle or as prominent as you choose. You may want to show off keepsakes from a close relative, such as your grandmother's wedding gloves or your mother's cake topper. Perhaps you love a cascading bouquet like those once carried by brides of another era.

By filling the wedding with nostalgic details, your day will have more meaning for you and your guests.

(Left) Whether it is given new or it once belonged to a beloved relative, an heirloom handkerchief is a sentimental touch when wrapped around the bouquet. If duty calls, the handkerchief can be used to quickly wipe away tears.

(Opposite page) By using flowers such as heirloom roses in table arrangements, the décor immediately takes on a vintage feel.

The Art of Calligraphy

For thousands of years, calligraphy has been an expressive script in cultures throughout the world. Decades ago, we rediscovered this fine art of penmanship when handwritten correspondence was the norm for weddings and other important occasions.

A professional calligrapher can be costly, yet there are ways to reduce the expense without sacrificing the distinctive scrolls and elaborate lettering befitting invitations, save-the-date cards, menus, and place cards.

If you haven't been trained in the fine art of calligraphy, there are countless people who have, or you might enjoy taking a calligraphy class. Rather than hand write each invitation, a master copy of the invitation can be professionally reproduced on quality paper, resulting in a memorable and eloquent request for your guest's presence.

When it comes to smaller stationery pieces such as place cards, experiment with printing your guests' names from your computer, using one of the many calligraphy fonts available.

(Above) In designing a vintage-style wedding, make details reminiscent of something old, including the type fonts on all correspondence.

(Opposite page) Tone-on-tone ecru invitations and announcements are a classic old-time approach to building a wedding theme.

We hope you will be able
to share our special day.

Please Save The Date of
March 16, 2002
for the wedding of
Meredith Barr Holly
to
Blake David Edwards

Meredith
and
Blake

Bride Ideas
Bouquet Etiquette

Some important things to remember when holding your bridal bouquet:

- Round, heart, cascade, and crescent bouquets are normally carried in front, low enough to reveal the details of the neckline and bodice of the bride's gown. The bouquet is held with both hands and arms rest at the hips.

- Small, lightweight, and delicate bouquets such as nosegays, clutch bouquets, or single blossoms can be carried to the side with one hand and are generally held at the same level as a bouquet held in front.

- If the nosegay is mounted in an elaborate tussy mussy, consider displaying it in the front rather than the side. To hold it properly, carry the tussy mussy upwards with the forearm bent so it is horizontal (parallel to the floor), while the elbow rests on the hip.

- Floral pomanders (bloom-covered balls or cones suspended from a ribbon) can be carried to the side or in front.

- Arm bouquets feature long floral stems and should rest cradled in the inner bend of the elbow with the blossom end of the flowers facing away from the body.

Bridal Bouquets

Every flower has a special meaning, which means the blooms chosen for the bouquet can say a lot about your love and relationship.

If you're enamored with the Victorian era, consider carrying a nosegay, a small, round cluster of aromatic flowers with lots of greenery and ribbon streamers. Nosegays can be carried in a family heirloom or reproduction tussy mussy, which is a small, Victorian-style metal or glass cone-shaped holder.

The cascade bouquet is a traditional, sophisticated choice. The elongated style is full and abundant, with blossoms at the top of the bouquet that taper downwards with flowing foliage, floral streamers, or ribbons at the bottom.

(Top and opposite page) A vintage-style bridal bouquet tends to be larger than others and is arranged in a cascade. To complete the look, choose classic flowers that have been used in weddings for many years.

Boutonnieres

Whether artificial or live flowers, it's important that the blooms selected for the groom's boutonniere reflect one of the prominent flowers in the bridal bouquet.

Incorporating holly for a winter wedding sends a message of domestic happiness; or in the spring, stephanotis speaks a similar message of marital bliss. The peony, a vintage favorite, brings wishes of a happy marriage and prosperity, while the pansy, when given by a man, sends pleasant thoughts and asks the woman to "think of me."

Boutonnieres are a wonderful way to add vintage touches such as handkerchiefs, fabric, ribbon, or even loose pearls. Here, something borrowed can be just as sentimental for the groom as for the bride.

(Opposite page, from top left) Tiny yellow narcissus and small white flowers are reminiscent of Victorian times. Paper flowers set on a swatch of fabric coordinates the groomsmen's boutonnieres with the bridal party attire. Paper flowers have a vintage feel and are pretty when tucked into a miniature paper pocket. White silk flowers and pearls make a traditional combination.

Flower Girl Accents

A sweet reminder of yesteryear can become part of a wedding in so many unexpected ways. Hearkening back to Victorian times, you can fashion a small pouch befitting the small hands of a flower girl.

In one example a lace handkerchief was used, while in another, a piece of sentimental silk fabric was chosen. The material was folded in half diagonally, and sewn at one edge. Once turned right side out, the carrier pouch or purse may be embellished with ribbon and artificial flowers. A 12" length of ribbon sewn at each side of the purse provides a delicate handle.

Once complete, the purse can be filled with flower petals, candy, tissues, or rice. After the wedding, the thoughtful purse becomes a gift for your flower girl to have and to hold.

(Right) A vintage handkerchief is lined and sewn into a small purse for a flower girl. The purse can be embellished with silk flowers, beads, or pearls.

(Opposite page) Heirloom fabric can be made into a purse for any female member of the wedding party. A purse made from a treasured dress or other piece of clothing from a previous celebration in the family can be a sentimental addition to the day.

Bridal Gloves and Veils

Evoking a more formal air, gloves fit in perfectly with traditional bridal attire. Gloves are available in a range of lengths—from wrist to elbow to over-the-elbow—and a selection of materials including satin, silk, lace, and spandex gloves in white, cream, and ivory are commonly available.

Grandmother's wedding gloves are a sentimental touch, or if you picked up a simple pair at an estate sale or second-hand shop, consider making them your own with beautiful trim and pearl accents easily attached with glue or simple stitches.

A headband is a wonderful match for a light-weight veil. While you may choose simple white, there are endless decorative ribbons—some with beads, others with pearls—that create stunning accessories. Also, consider covering the headband with fabric gathered or pleated, then layering with your elements of choice.

(Above) Often a mother or grandmother has saved the gloves from her wedding. Consider adding some beaded trim. If your gown doesn't work well with gloves, they can be part of a heartfelt vignette.

(Opposite page) Veils are available in many lengths and styles in the wedding section of a craft store. A vintage-style wedding often calls for a luxurious, long veil. You may wish to attach the veil to the headpiece with hook-and-loop tape so that it can be detached during the reception.

Receiving Table

When planning a wedding, chances are you'll need a lot of table space. The grandest display should be the receiving table, where presents and a receptacle for cards are placed.

When planning for a vintage-style wedding, there's special room for something old—whether picked up on your own or a cherished family heirloom.

For an unforgettable box to hold cards, cover a plain box with vintage lace. Be sure to cut a slit long enough to accommodate even the largest envelopes along the top. Attach fabric with spray adhesive and add a lace border at the edges for interest. Finishing touches can include vintage photos, an old handkerchief, and a tulle bow. A box so pretty can be displayed in your home after the festivities.

(Top right and right) An exquisite box for gift cards is simple to make using fabric, spray adhesive, and a sturdy box. Cover lid separately so the box can be opened easily. Glue trim and ribbon around the edges of the lid.

(Opposite page) Take extra care to dress up the receiving table for the occasion. Organza and tulle make a lovely table cover, and often can be used again.

An Easy, Elegant Display

Materials:

- 18" x 24" piece of foam core
- 1.5 yards of fabric
- 1.5 yards of batting
- 4 yards of ribbon
- Frame with 18" x 24" opening
- Hot glue gun

To make:

1. Carefully remove glass from frame.

2. Cover foam core with batting, using hot glue gun.

3. Cover batting with fabric. Measure and cut fabric about 2" longer than foam core on all four sides. Glue 2" overage to reverse side of foam core.

4. Cut lengths of ribbon about 4" longer than width of foam core. Arrange ribbon in even rows over fabric. Be sure to allow for height of place cards. Glue ribbons to reverse side of foam core using 2" on each side.

5. Glue bottom edge of each ribbon to fabric to create a pocket for place cards.

6. Finish reverse side of foam core by covering with a decorative paper or fabric. Place foam core in frame.

Place Card Holder

Just as pretty as the place cards themselves is a stately decorative frame designed to hold the cards. The frame can be purchased in many styles, or you may choose to spray paint new life into an old frame that has suffered some wear and tear. Using a similar technique for creating a memo board, you can make a dramatic focal point.

- Be sure to select fabric and ribbon that will offer a subtle backdrop to avoid detracting from the place cards themselves.

- If the ribbon is not quite taut enough, adhere a small bead of museum wax to the back of each place card to ensure they keep their place.

- Once the honeymoon is over, the frame can be used to frame your wedding portrait.

(Opposite page) A place card holder is a museum-quality display, and very easy to make using a store-bought picture frame. After the wedding, the backing can be reinserted and the frame used in the bride and groom's new home.

Table Settings

Once guests take their seats, a thoughtful gesture lends a wonderful surprise at the table setting.

Lace is reminiscent of days gone by, and makes a wonderful accent at each place setting. Lace can be easily adhered to the back side of a glass plate using a decoupage medium—a wonderful way to dress up an everyday, inexpensive piece of dinnerware.

Another way to add vintage flair is to feature the wedding photos of each guest at his and her place. A month before the wedding, ask each married guest for a copy of one of their wedding photos. Photocopy the photo in black and white and mount it on a sturdy piece of card stock. It doesn't matter if the wedding was two months or 20 years ago—the message of love promised and shared is the same.

(Right) A thoughtful gesture that is sure to make guests welcome at a wedding reception is to have a photo from their own wedding day at their place. It is also a great way to start conversations among guests who have not met before the reception.

(Opposite page) Beautiful lace can be adhered to the back of a glass plate to create an exquisite charger. You can use a decoupage medium or a liquid laminate product available at craft stores.

Quick Napkin Rings

Materials:

- 1 paper towel roll for every 7 rings, or 1 toilet paper roll for every 3 rings

- Embellishments such as loose pearls, pearl trim, ribbon, clusters of artificial flowers

- Enough fabric to cover rings

- Hot glue gun

- Spray glue

To make:

1. Slice paper rolls evenly so they are about 1½" wide to create ring.

2. Cut strips of fabric about 1" wider than roll and just about as long as roll.

3. Spray glue fabric, then adhere to ring.

4. Secure fabric to inside of ring with glue gun, if needed.

5. Attach embellishments to napkin ring with glue gun.

Napkin Rings

Elegant napkin rings don't have to come with a lofty price tag. In fact, common household items and simple embellishments are all that is needed to create one-of-a-kind napkin rings.

The blush hues of the bridesmaid dresses or another color significant to your special day can lead the way for this project. Some things you may have around the house—beaded trim, clusters of artificial flowers, or loose pearls—while others can easily be picked up at a craft store. Regardless of the items you choose, creative napkin rings are easy to make and fun to share.

(Above) Napkin rings are one of the little details that have the greatest impact in a table setting.

(Opposite page) All four napkins rings are made by covering and embellishing a toilet paper roll. Bits of fabric, ribbon, beaded and pearl trim, and small faux flowers can be used to decorate the rings. For a fun look, don't match the designs. Instead, work within a similar color palette and make each guest's napkin ring different.

Centerpieces

Just as the flowers for the bridal bouquet and boutonniere are carefully chosen, as much thought should be put into floral centerpieces.

Centerpieces are a delightful way to add old-time favorites such as heirloom roses, fresh hydrangea, and peonies. A colorful bouquet calls for a simple vase so it's best to choose one with a low profile for unobstructed views and easy conversation between guests.

If you collect old silverplate or ceramic pitchers, consider what beautiful and interesting vases they would make. Slightly nicked or dinged containers can be picked up for a song at second-hand or thrift shops. The unique centerpieces will garner so much attention that few will notice their imperfections.

(Right) A silver vase is an obvious choice for holding flowers for a vintage wedding. A spray metallic mirror finish can be easily applied to inexpensive plastic or glass vases to transform them to classic style.

(Opposite page) Centerpieces at a vintage wedding should be graceful. Tendrils of ivy and other greens spilling from the arrangement and brushing the table duplicates a soft Victorian style.

Paper Cone Project

To create a paper cone, you will need:

- 8½" by 11" lightweight decorative paper for outer shell
- 8½" by 11" heavyweight paper or favorite textured wallpaper for inner shell
- Ribbon strong enough to support paper cone when filled
- Rubber bands, plastic sandwich bags, ties
- Scissors, staples, clear tape, hot glue gun, hole punch

To make:

1. Place both papers together on flat surface, with heavyweight paper on top.

2. Roll paper into a cone. Staple, tape, or hot glue one end over another. Be sure papers are slightly offset so you can see at least 1" of inner paper peeking out.

3. Punch small hole on each side of cone with hole punch and pull ribbon through holes, securing on each side with a knot. Leave enough ribbon for cone to hang freely.

4. Gather freshly cut flowers in bunch, wrap wet paper towel around base of stems, and secure with rubber band; then place into a small plastic sandwich bag. Tie bag with elastic or twist tie. Place flowers in cone.

Paper Cones

Paper cones are blooming everywhere—down the aisles, on guest chairs, dangling from the head table where the bride and groom reign.

Cones are fanciful reminders of May Day, when traditional simple pockets filled with garden flowers and strung with ribbon were hung on doorknobs. What makes paper cones so perfect for a wedding is that they are easy—and inexpensive—to make. You can go simple—just add a sweet bow to the front—or go all out, layering paper embellishments. Remember that just about any paper will do, but handmade paper and cardstock are more durable choices.

Tuck in some flowers or fill the cones with candies for a wonderful take-home treat. Whatever your fancy, have a ball getting creative with paper.

(Opposite page) The decorative possibilities with paper cones are end-less. While any paper will work, the wide selection of handmade papers and vellums work best. Use a staple to secure the shape of the cone, and cover the staple with embellishments. For a dramatic effect, layer two or three papers.

Wedding Cakes

What makes a wedding cake take on a vintage theme are the elements used to accessorize it—from the cake topper to the cake-cutting knife and server, and any flowers used to decorate the table.

Ask your family and the groom's family if someone close to either of you has his or her own wedding cake topper tucked away. They would likely be flattered that you'd like to use it to mark your own wedding celebration. You or your fiancé may have a special keepsake that would be an appropriate and graceful touch to the cake.

Consider borrowing a grandmother's silver cake knife, or start your own tradition by having your wedding date engraved onto an antique cake server purchased for the occasion.

(Opposite page) Lace-like scroll work in white frosting evokes the grandeur of a bygone era. Cake-decorating tips available at craft stores make it easy to embellish a wedding cake.

Chapter Four

To Begin...

LOBSTER LOUIS PARFAIT
LOBSTER, TOMATO AND AVOCADO MOUSSE TOWER
WITH A CREAMY LIME DRESSING

Second Course

SALAD GOURMANDISE
LIMESTONE LETTUCE, BABY ARUGULA, AND MICRO SPROUTS
TOSSED WITH AN AGED BALSAMIC VINAIGRETTE
ROUGIE FOIE GRAS TERRINE, ARTICHOKE CRISPS,
EDIBLE FLOWERS, AND CANDIED PECANS

CHEESE TOAST AND TWISTS
SEEDED FLAT BREAD AND POPPADUMS

Entrée

BEEF TENDERLOIN TOURNEDOES
WITH A BAROLO WINE SAUCE
SAGE POTATO GRATIN
CRISPY LEEKS
STILTON CHEESECAKE TARTLET
ROASTED ASPARAGUS SPEARS WITH RED AND
ORANGE CHERRY TOMATOES

ASSORTED BREADS AND ROLLS

Dessert

OUR WEDDING CAKE
FRESH FRUIT & ARTISANAL CHEESE DISPLAY
SELECTION OF HEART-SHAPED COOKIES AND TREATS
SORBET & GELATO STATION
COFFEE AND TEA

Champagne Taste

Black-tie formal means a wedding both elegant and sophisticated.

Many of us have a small budget and big, fairy-tale dreams. A wedding can be an endless round of payments with everyone from the caterer to the florist holding out their hands as they promise the perfect setting. If you aren't careful, before you know it, you'll be spending your first-born's college fund.

The truth is, you can have the wedding of your dreams without breaking the bank, even if your champagne taste calls for a formal affair.

Forget the crystal and go for the glass; think silver and opt for a can of spray paint; and above all, be sure there is plenty of candlelight in the room. Keep it elegant and you will be surprised at how stunning—and affordable—your celebration can become.

(Left) Use the standard plates, flatware, and glassware the caterer provides to save money, and spend on the special touches such as a personalized menu or note at each place.

(Opposite page) Glitter and glimmer are the trademarks of a champagne wedding reception. The challenge is to get the glitz without the price tag.

Wedding Invitations

Invitations don't have to be large to be fancy. By keeping them small, you can save money on paper and postage.

Dressy affairs usually mean sophisticated touches. So when it comes to a formal wedding, think shimmer and shine. Before putting the invitation into an envelope, embellish a sheer organza bag with small rhinestones affixed in a fanciful pattern. Inside, the same rhinestones are glued down the side of the ecru wedding invitation. All that's needed is an envelope and a few stamps.

Save the Date

What better way to celebrate your good taste than with a bottle of champagne? With custom-made labels, a bottle of champagne becomes a creative way to announce impending nuptials.

A dimensional label can be made with decorative craft paper cut in various sizes and adhered with spray glue. Two ribbons wrapped around three pieces of the layered papers are held in place with a stick-on label that can be printed from a home computer. A pretty tulle bow makes the perfect finishing touch.

(Top and above) Small organza gift bags embellished with rhinestones are called into duty as a sparkling cover for invitations.

(Opposite page) A personalized wine bottle is a creative way to announce your upcoming nuptials and invite a close friend to be in the wedding party.

Save the date
Priscilla and Gregory
Saturday
September 4

Hand Tie Your Bouquet

Note: Be sure to choose fresh flowers.

Materials:

- 2 dozen roses
- 5 yards of ribbon (1½" or wider)
- Floral wire
- Sharp gardening pruning sheers

To make:

1. Build arrangement in your hand so all flower heads are even, layered along side of each other at an angle.

2. Turn arrangement slightly at stems for a soft, twisted effect.

3. For a loose bouquet, keep more leaves on stems. For a tight bouquet, take off more.

4. Using your free hand, wrap floral wire around stems, just under flower heads. Trim stems so they're about 6" or 7" long.

5. To wrap ribbon around stems, begin at top. Leave enough length at top to tie bow. Wrap ribbon at 45-degree angle.

6. When you reach the bottom, begin to wrap back upwards at 45-degree angle. Double-wrap stems if necessary.

7. Wrap ribbon to top. Tie loose ends in a bow. Cut ends of ribbons diagonally.

Bridal Bouquets

Roses are by far the most popular choice of flowers for bouquets. When it comes to a formal affair, especially one held at night, introducing a striking color such as red really steps up the drama.

A cluster of beautiful roses, hand tied at the stems, is a beautiful option befitting an elegant bride. Roses are especially sentimental, bringing a message of unity and romantic love. While roses are not the most economical choice, interspersing silk roses throughout the bouquet of primarily live flowers can lower the cost.

If you want to preserve your bouquet, consider using all artificial roses in your arrangement.

(Top and opposite page) Roses speak for themselves when gathered and hand tied in a simple bouquet. Whether you choose to have the stems exposed or covered with ribbon or fabric is a personal choice. Just be sure that there is nothing on the stems that can stain the dress.

Boutonnieres

When it comes to the groom's boutonniere, a traditional red rose is stunning—or you can go with something less traditional and much more dynamic.

Thinking outside the flower box will make an impact and open up the choices considerably. Mixing interesting elements including fresh rosemary, a feather, or a spray of dried flowers are just a few ideas.

Remember the season. In spring you're likely to find rannunculus, sweet peas, and lilies; summer is perfect for roses and lilies; in fall you can find sunflowers, winter jasmine, and zinnias; and winter is best for chrysanthemums and dahlias.

Also, by choosing a flower or elements with a burst of color you won't need an elaborate display—just a happy groom with a austere lapel.

(Opposite page) Fresh herbs, such as rosemary, mix well in a boutonniere and will bring a pleasant aroma to the day. Unconventional flowers and leaves can make a boutonniere a conversation piece.

Flower Girl Accents

The last thing you want to do is spend a fortune on shoes—for both you and the flower girl. Many times, the shoes are worn once and not long after the wedding, they're relegated to the old clothes pile and donated to charity.

It makes perfect sense to keep shoes simple, with an equally non-flashy price, and embellish them to make them a delight to wear. Flowers, ribbon, decorative trim, and a hot glue gun are all that's needed to make a plain pair of shoes fancy. Be sure to use high-temperature glue sticks to ensure that embellishments stay in place until after the last dance. You may wish to stitch trims in place for more staying power.

Bridal Veils

If a wedding is formal, it's expected that all involved dress up a notch. It's befitting to wear a tiara, which can be gussied up with fancy trim and attached to a veil with a hot glue gun or heavy white thread.

Tiaras can be found in craft stores and typically are not expensive. The look is befitting any princess on her special day.

(Above) White ballet slippers trimmed with pearls and silk flowers are a lovely accent to a flower girl's dress. Replace the elastic band on the slippers with a satin ribbon.

(Opposite page) Tiaras are worthy of the most elegant of brides—and despite their traditionally over-the-top appeal, they don't have to cost a fortune.

Receiving Table

The receiving table sets the tone for the wedding reception. A table dressed in a dramatic black, white, and red color scheme can be complemented by a silver vase of loose flowers. The purity of the day is represented in an elegant wood frame, which is a standard wood frame and a museum mat customized when stenciled with pewter paint for a rich effect.

(Left and above) The brush stroke characters on the white handmade paper translate into the word, "happiness." What better way to describe the special day? Wrap special thank-you gifts and set them on the receiving table before the wedding and direct your biggest helpers to them.

(Opposite page) Bold color is striking, so don't be afraid to use the reddest red if it is your favorite color.

Party Poppers in a Snap!

While these crackers don't feature the signature "snap" of a traditional cracker, they are just as lovely as the real thing.

Materials:

- 1 toilet tissue roll per cracker
- 8" x 10" piece of crepe paper
- 2 pieces of 8" x 5" crepe paper
- Decorative string or ribbon
- Decorative trimmings
- Glue
- Small favors to place inside
- Transparent tape

To make:

1. Center tissue roll lengthwise along edge of 10" side of crepe paper. Wrap crepe paper around roll, securing it with 1 or 2 pieces of tape at underside of paper. Insert favors inside roll.

2. Tie each end of cracker with string or ribbon.

3. To make fringe, fold 8" x 5" piece of crepe paper in half lengthwise.

4. Take about 12" of decorative string or ribbon and place along inside fold of fringe. Gather and tie around end of cracker, over first tie. Repeat with other end, using second sheet of crepe paper.

Party Favors

Party crackers are a favorite way to celebrate the holidays and special occasions. These traditional party favors are tube-like containers embellished with decorative papers. They are tied at the ends and filled with candy or other treats. Typically, a "snap" is heard when the ends are pulled off to open the cracker.

Easy to make, crackers are a great way to tie in the color—and the ambience—of your wedding.

Asian-inspired handmade paper, along with a sheet of red paper and some tissue paper, create a festive cracker. The paper can be as sophisticated as you like, and is easily tied at each end with a pretty ribbon or decorative cording.

(Opposite page) Party crackers are a festive way to get everyone talking when they first sit down to the table at the reception. While the homemade version may not snap, they can be filled with many different fun trinkets that are sure to bring smiles.

Shopping for a Florist

Most brides spend 5 to 10 percent of their budget on flowers, and an additional 10 to 20 percent more for delivery and set up. Some things to remember when pricing your arrangements:

- Get quotes from multiple florists. Be sure the product is worth the price.

- Be sure the quote includes delivery charges and taxes.

- Containers can be a big expense; ask your florist about renting them.

- Use in-season, locally grown flowers.

- Fill the arrangement with lots of greenery.

Floral Centerpieces

When it comes to wedding expenses, flowers can take up a significant portion of your budget. This is especially true if you hire a florist to create elaborate centerpieces for each of the guest tables.

While you can save money by making the centerpieces yourself, there are savings in the types of flowers you choose. A striking centerpiece of roses, orchids, and lilies may sound divine, but it comes with a significant price tag.

To keep costs down, consider flowers that are lower in price such as freesia and gerbera daisies. If you've just got to have lilies, consider adding just one or two to the arrangement, or using less-expensive lilies in place of top-of-the-line Siberia lilies.

Party Favors

If your arrangements are blooming with color and interest, you can get away with simple party favors. Opt for store-bought boxes such as ones shaped to look like small tuxedos. Filled with candy, the boxes reflect the sophisticated flavor of the wedding.

(Left) Craft stores are filled with creative boxes that double as party favors, such as these tuxedos ideal for a formal affair.

(Opposite page) Tones of gold and red blend well. Low floral arrangements, colored ribbon ties on napkins, and votive candles create a warm glow.

Napkin Folding

An inexpensive way to dress up a table and show fine taste is with elegantly folded napkins. By following a few easy instructions, napkins are fun to fold and best of all, they don't require napkin rings.

The Blooming Flower

1. Position napkin diagonally in front of you. Fold into a triangle.
2. Fold each side up to middle to form a diagonal square.
3. Fold lower portion over to the top of the square to form a triangle.
4. Fold the tip of the upper layer back to the lower edge.
5. Tuck the left and right corners into each other in the back. Pull down both upper tips to make a leaf effect.

The Lotus

1. Position napkin in front of you and fold all four corners into the middle.
2. Turn napkin over and again fold all corners to the middle.
3. Pull out the tips that are underneath the four corners.
4. Continue with the inside tips. Hold the middle with one hand as you pull.
5. Finish by placing flowers or other decoration in the center of the finished design.

The Tuxedo

1. Position napkin diagonally in front of you. Fold into a triangle.
2. Fold lower edge up about 1".
3. Turn napkin over and fold each upper corner down to middle.
4. Fold sides back to create jacket shape.
5. Finish jacket by folding lower edge under. Decorate with a ribbon to make the tie.

The Water Lily

1. Follow the first two steps of the Lotus.
2. While holding the center of the napkin down, carefully pull out the four corners.
3. Place flowers, place cards, or favors in the middle of the design.

(Opposite page, from top left) The Blooming Flower, The Lotus, The Tuxedo, and The Water Lily are spectacular napkin-folding techniques that are easy and interesting.

Candle Centerpieces

Candle centerpieces are a great way to stretch a budget while still decorating beautifully. Candlelight is spectacular both indoors and out, and offers lovely reflections on a table set with glass and silver.

Not only do similar candles set a romantic mood, they are also very decorative. Candles themselves are relatively inexpensive, and if you are on the lookout, you're sure to find bargains galore.

Choose one thick candle for a centerpiece, or a cluster of various sized candles for more impact. Candles can be set on individual low holders, or grouped on a tray or mirror.

(Above) Candles can be embellished in many ways. Pearl or beaded trim looks elegant affixed to the rim of a large candle. White craft glue adheres well and does not melt the wax the way a glue gun will.

(Right) Stickers designed for scrapbooking are easily attached to candles and are quick to apply.

(Opposite page) A trio of embellished candles adds ambience to a table and is a fraction of the cost of floral arrangements.

Champagne Flutes

On such a special occasion, every bride and groom needs a special glass to toast their good fortune.

A basic pair of flutes, whether crystal or glass, can be given the royal treatment with some finishing touches. Hand-painted designs and simple bows also offer personalized detailing at a small price. Consider wrapping the stem of flutes with beautiful satin ribbon or embellishing the base with a small cluster of artificial flowers. Easy to make ahead of the wedding, dressy champagne flutes are a fine dining detail.

(Left) A champagne toast is a tradition at most weddings, and the glasses have become sentimental keepsakes for years to come. Rather than spend a fortune on fine crystal, there are many ways to decorate glass flutes.

(Opposite page, from top left) A strand of faux pearls wound around the stem of the glasses is held in place with craft glue and finished with ribbon flowers; to further personalize the glasses, an etching medium was used to put a design on the glass. Glass paint comes in many colors, making it possible to paint any motif including blooming roses on glassware. Flutes can be adorned with vintage ribbon, and decorated with rub-on glass transfer designs. Simple decoration is a small tulle bow tied on each glass.

Wedding Cakes

An elegant wedding celebration calls for a stunning cake. But don't worry; you can pull this off and stay within your budget.

A beautiful cake doesn't mean elaborate frosting designs and out-of-season berries as the filling. Keeping it simple can have elegant results. A plain white cake with minimal detailing can be dressed with a few small red and white flowers accented with a couple of leaves.

When it comes to the cake, another cost is the topper. Many store-bought toppers are available, and some bakeries even rent theirs. You can get creative and come up with a topper that represents the two of you as a couple.

If you have a cake, you'll need a cake-cutting knife and server. While these can be picked up for a song, you may want to dress them up with a couple of small blooms and satin ribbon. They not only make sophisticated accessories, they will look great in your wedding photos.

(Right) Incorporate a favorite figurine—such as glass swans or a porcelain statue—as your wedding cake topper. If you don't have a favorite, ask a beloved relative to loan hers.

(Opposite page) A simple dash of color is all that is needed to bring some drama to a stately wedding cake with simple scrolls.

Your Perfect Day

The most important detail of any wedding day are the vows you make and your commitment to go forward into life as a team. There is no need to add the stress of going over budget on your wedding to the challenges of a new marriage. With careful planning, a little creativity, and the helping hands of family and friends, you can have the wedding of your dreams...and a life lived happily ever after.

Acknowledgments

Calligraphy/Shower Invitations
Janet Takahashi, Torrance, CA

Designers/projects
www.victorianboutique.com
Mary Boulais
Michel Smoley

Etching medium, paint, paper punches, rubber stamps,
stencils, and transfers
Plaid Enterprises
www.plaidonline.com

Favors, ribbon, ring pillow, silk flowers, trims, tiaras,
tulle, and veils
Hirshberg Shutz Co., Inc.
Available at Michaels and other quality craft stores

Florist
Taka
Be Buds Florist
www.bebuds.com

Frame
Aaron Brothers
www.aaronbrothers.com

Glue gun, sealing wax, and seals
Kirk & Matz Limited
www.kirk-matz.com

Invitations/Save-the-Date cards
The Oak and the Acorn
www.theoakandtheacorn.com

Papers and embellishments
Loose Ends
www.looseends.com

Trims
Flights of Fancy
www.flightsoffancyboutique.com

Thank you to Lon and Kathy Hurwitz for the invitation
to photograph at their beautiful home.

Photography Credits

Belle 'n' Beau
Raymond H. Elgin, photographer
Pages 28, 36, 52, 92, 99, 114-115

Doug Gifford
www.douggiffordphoto.com
Pages 3, 30, 46, 52, 104, 120

Ryne Hazen
Ogden, Utah
Page 89

Denny Nelson
www.dennynelson.com
Pages 2, 4, 6, 12-19, 23, 25, 27, 31-35, 37-39, 41-42, 45, 48-51, 53, 55-63, 71, 73-76, 78-83, 86-87, 91, 93, 95, 97, 100-103, 105-111, 113, 117-119, 121-128

Laurie Ann Martin
www.laurieannmartinphotography.com
Pages 8-11, 24

Bradley Olman
www.bradleyolman.com
Pages 20-21, 29, 40, 43, 54, 56, 70

Mark Tanner
www.marktannergallery.com
Pages 64-69, 76-77, 84-85, 90, 94

Our sincere appreciation to Wilton Enterprises, www.wilton.com, for the images of their magnificent cakes on pages 47, 72

Index